(BOOK TWO)

THE
SPIRIT-FILLED
CHRISTIAN

NAVPRESS®

BRINGING TRUTH TO LIFE

OUR GUARANTEE TO YOU

The Navigators is an international Christian organization. Our mission is to reach, disciple, and equip people to know Christ and to make Him known through successive generations. We envision multitudes of diverse people in the United States and every other nation who have a passionate love for Christ, live a lifestyle of sharing Christ's love, and multiply spiritual laborers among those without Christ.

NavPress is the publishing ministry of The Navigators. NavPress publications help believers learn biblical truth and apply what they learn to their lives and ministries. Our mission is to stimulate spiritual formation among our readers.

NAVPRESS, BRINGING TRUTH TO LIFE, and the NAVPRESS logo are registered trademarks of NavPress. Absence of ® in connection with marks of NavPress or other parties does not indicate an absence of registration of those marks.

FOR A FREE CATALOG OF
NAVPRESS BOOKS & BIBLE STUDIES,
CALL 1-800-366-7788 (USA)
OR 1-416-499-4615 (CANADA)

HELPING YOU LEARN

Have you realized that you have a personal tutor at your side as you study the Bible? He is always available to help you understand what it means and how it applies to you. He is the Author of the Bible—the Holy Spirit. Jesus Christ said the Holy Spirit would "teach you all things," and "guide you into all truth" (John 14:26; 16:13).

The Holy Spirit teaches you both in your personal study of the Bible and as you listen to God-appointed pastors and teachers. One is not a substitute for the other—you need both personal study and the teaching of others.

Ask for the Spirit's guidance as you study. Psalm 119:18 is a good prayer: "Open my eyes that I may see wonderful things in your law."

For your personal Bible study, you need:

- A time: Just as church attendance is planned for a regular time each week, you should also plan a time for your Bible study. Some like to study a little every day; others set aside an evening each week. Decide on a time that is best for you, then stick to it faithfully.
- A place: If possible, choose a place free from distractions.
- Method: As you look up each verse of Scripture, think about it carefully, then write out your answer. It's also helpful to read the context (the surrounding verses) of each passage listed. Write the answers in your own words whenever possible.
- Material: Beside your study book, you will need a complete Bible—Old and New Testaments.

In Book One, *Your Life in Christ,* you discovered the reasons for the central place Christ holds in your life. But you may have wondered, *How do I live a Spirit-filled, Christ-centered life?* In this study you will find answers to this question in five important areas:

- The Obedient Christian
- God's Word in Your Life
- Conversing with God
- Fellowship with Christians
- Witnessing for Christ

CHAPTER ONE

THE OBEDIENT CHRISTIAN

At the moment you placed your faith in Jesus Christ as your Savior, a life of obedience to God became a real possibility. The Holy Spirit set you free from the bondage of sin and death (Romans 8:2). He enables you to live a Christlike life.

> *"It is not just that we should strive to live like Jesus, but that Jesus by his Spirit should come and live in us. To have him as our example is not enough; we need him as our Savior. It is thus through his atoning death that the penalty of our sins may be forgiven; whereas it is through his indwelling Spirit that the power of our sins may be broken."*

—JOHN R. W. STOTT*

As you learn more about the obedient Christian in action, remember that the Holy Spirit will help you obey.

THE BASIS FOR OBEDIENCE

When you consider obedience to God, it is necessary to remember who he is and what he desires for you.

1. What do the following statements tell you about God?

a. *1 John 4:8* _____ God is love _____

b. *Revelation 4:11* _____ God created all things for His pleasure _____

*From *Basic Christianity* (London: Inter-Varsity Christian Fellowship, 1958), page 105.

c. How do these facts influence your obedience to God?

That we should love us he loved - the desire to obey Him out of love

2. Read Deuteronomy 10:12-13   *328*

a. What did God require from Israel?

To fear Him and to love Him and obey

b. Why did God desire that they keep these commandments?

for your own good.

c. How does this apply to a Christian today?

The same as it did back then

3. What does 1 John 5:3 teach about God's commandments?

To love God is to obey His commandments

4. After reflecting on John 14:15 and 14:21, briefly state the relationship between loving God and obeying him.

It's one of the same to love Him is to obey them to obey Him is to love Him

OBEDIENCE TO GOD

How do you know what God desires for your life? The Bible is God's revelation of truth, and obedience to God's word is obedience to God himself.

1164

5. Psalm 119 deals with the importance of God's word. What are several ways the Bible can help you live for Christ?

Verse 11 _To hide his Love in your heart_

1169 Verse 105 _His word shows us the path we should take_

1170 Verse 130 _it help us to understand_

2333 **6.** In 2 Timothy 3:16 Paul said that the Scriptures are profitable for: _inspiration - Doctor_

a. _Believe and follow scripture_ (What to believe and do)

b. _Rebuking Scripture_ (Recognizing sin)

c. _Correcting + training_ (How to change)

d. _By following God and loving Him_ (How to live)

This can be illustrated in the following manner:

TEACHING
Shows you the path
to walk on.

TRAINING IN RIGHTEOUSNESS
Shows you how to stay
on the path.

CORRECTION
Shows you how to get
back on the path.

REPROOF
Shows you where you've
gotten off the path.

7

7. Jesus presents a vivid picture of two types of people in Matthew 7:24-27: the wise man and the foolish man. Read the passage and answer the following questions.

	WISE MAN	FOOLISH MAN
On what foundation was the house built?	_upon the rock_	_upon the sand_
To what forces were both houses exposed?	_rain, wind, flood_	
What was the result?	_the rock stood solid_	_the sand fell_
Did this person hear God's word?	_yes_	_yes_

How did these two men differ?

The wiseman put His words into practice and the foolish man listened, but did not follow His word

8. Perhaps God's word has recently made you aware of an area of your life which needs to be brought into closer obedience to God. If so, in what area?

We need to follow His Words

KEYS TO CONSISTENT OBEDIENCE

God's Provision

God does not expect you to live an obedient life in your own strength. He has provided you with everything necessary to make obedience a reality.

9. Who lives in every believer?

1 Corinthians 3:16 _Gods Spirit_

2 Corinthians 6:16 _Our Body which is His Temple_

Galatians 2:20 _His Son died for us._

8

10. Why are Christians able to overcome their enemy in the world? *1 John 4:4*

The Holy Spirit lives in us and He is greater than the spirit of world

2412

11. In addition to his personal presence, what else has God given to help you live for him? Match the letter with the appropriate reference.

2330   _C_ *2 Timothy 1:7*   a. All things that pertain to life and godliness

2398   _a_ *2 Peter 1:3*   b. The Scriptures

2193   _b_ *Romans 15:4*   c. Power, love, and self-control

Your Attitudes

While God has equipped you for obedience, a key to successful use of these resources is your attitude.

12. What attitudes can you display in obeying God?

350   *Deuteronomy 26:16*   *to follow His decrees and laws*

1051   *Psalm 40:8*   *to do His will with all our heart and sole*

1974   *Luke 8:15*   *by hearing and preserving His word*

THE PRACTICE OF OBEDIENT LIVING

The obedient Christian still faces daily struggles with temptation. How can we practice obedience and gain victory over sin? Biblical principles and examples provide the answer.

13. Discover the source and causes of temptation in the following verses:

a. Who is the tempter? *Matthew 4:1-3*

839   *The devil*

2375 b. Who is never the source of temptation? *James 1:13*

_____God_____

c. What causes you to be drawn into temptation? *James 1:14*

by our own desires - which guides hurt to sin

382 **14.** In Joshua 7:20-21, examine Achan's statement about his disobedience.

a. What factors contributed to his disobedience?

sining against the Lord plunder, robe. 200 shekels of silver a wedge of Gold weighs 50 shekles

b. At what point could he have prevented his sin?

If he had listened to Gods comand through Joshua

c. What can you learn from his error?

If we error we will regret it later

15. Using the following verses as a guide, write a brief definition of sin. *Isaiah 53:6; James 4:17; 1 John 3:4*

1396   2378   24/1   2469

When you do something against Gods will.

10

How does sin differ from temptation? _____

temptation is thinking about
doing something — sin is
do it!

_____

16. Consider 1 Corinthians 10:13.

a. Are the temptations you face different and perhaps more difficult than those faced by others?

No.

b. What limit does God place on temptation?

What we can bear

_____

c. What is God sure to provide when you are tempted?

a way so we can stand
under it. a way we can escape.

This verse is a promise to claim. If you memorize and review it, it will remind you to look for the way out when you are tempted.

God offers us victory and deliverance, but men sin because they often neglect the provision. Known but unconfessed sin grieves God. Although sin does not alter God's love, it does cause a break in fellowship with him.

17. In 1 John 1:9 we are told to. . .(Check the correct answer.)

____feel badly about sin.

____try to do something to make up for sin.

✓ confess sin to God.

____try to forget about sin.

Why is this important? *He is faith*
to forgive if we confess
our sin

11

1038

18. In Psalm 32:5, David prays and confesses his sin. Write this verse in your own words.

I will confess my sins to the Lord and ask his forgiveness — and he will forgive me

The practice of walking in victory can be pictured as follows:

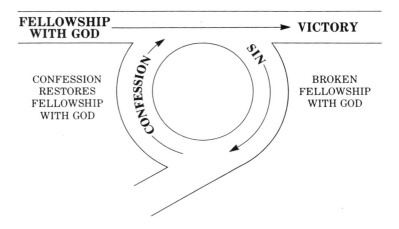

1209 **19.** In what practical ways can you avoid falling into temptation? *Proverbs 4:13-15*

By obeying His instructions (the scripture/commandment

2399

20. What two steps indicated in James 4:7 will help you walk in victory? *to God*

Submit and Resist Devil

TO SUBMIT TO GOD you must yield your will to God's will. TO RESIST THE DEVIL you must use God's provision for victory.

21. These questions about sin and temptation probably remind you of the daily conflict you experience.

a. Review question 8. What is the root problem in the area you recorded?

by trying to do it our way and not His way

b. How does the temptation to disobey God in this area begin to show itself?

By the stress of our daily life

c. What steps can you take to avoid these beginnings?

Walking with God.

"Live by the Spirit, and you will not gratify the desires of your sinful nature."

—GALATIANS 5:16

Remember These Points:

- Your obedience to God is based on the fact that he is your Creator. You obey him because of who he is.
- God reveals his standards through the Scriptures.
- To the extent that you appropriate God's provision for victory, you can experience a life of obedience.
- You are not immune, however, from temptation and sin. Sin does not negate God's love for you, but it does break your fellowship with him. Confession restores that fellowship.

CHAPTER TWO

GOD'S WORD IN YOUR LIFE

A sword is to be used skillfully in battle as both an offensive and a defensive weapon. God has equipped you with such a weapon for your spiritual battle: "the sword of the Spirit, which is the word of God" (Ephesians 6:17). The Holy Spirit uses the word of God to accomplish the work of God.

> *"The great need of the hour among persons spiritually hungry is twofold: first, to know the Scriptures, apart from which no saving truth will be vouchsafed by our Lord; the second, to be enlightened by the Spirit, apart from whom the Scriptures will not be understood."*
>
> —A. W. TOZER*

GOD'S WORD— HIS COMMUNICATION TO YOU

The Bible is the most remarkable book ever written. The writing was done by about forty men of many occupations. They wrote over a period of approximately 1,500 years, and in three languages—Hebrew, Aramaic, and Greek. Yet the Bible has one great theme and central figure—Jesus Christ. All of this would be impossible unless the Bible had one supreme Author—and it did: the Holy Spirit of God.

1. What does 2 Timothy 3:16 say about the Scriptures? (Circle the letter of the correct answer.)

*From *The Root of the Righteous* (Harrisburg, Pennsylvania: Christian Publications, 1955), page 37.

a. Some of the Bible is inspired by God.
b. All of it is inspired by God.
c. Only the parts that speak to you in a personal way are inspired by God.

Inspired comes from a Greek word meaning "God-breathed."

> "The meaning, then, is not that God breathed into the writers, nor that he somehow breathed into the writings to give them their special character, but that what was written by men was breathed out by God. He spoke through them. They were his spokesmen."

1544

—JOHN R. W. STOTT*

2. How was Scripture given? *2 Peter 1:20-21*

through men, as they spoke as they were moved by the Holy Spirit

Who, then, helps you understand the Bible?
1 Corinthians 2:12-13 *139 3*

the spirit who is from God

THE BIBLE AT A GLANCE (66 BOOKS)

OLD TESTAMENT (39 books)			"The New is in the Old concealed. The Old is in the New revealed."		NEW TESTAMENT (27 books)		
HISTORY 17 books	**POETRY** 5 books	**PROPHECY** 17 books			**HISTORY** 5 books	**TEACHING** 21 books	**PROPHECY** 1 book
Law	Job	**Major prophets**			**Gospels**	**Paul's letters**	Revelation
Genesis	Psalms	Isaiah			Matthew	Romans	
Exodus	Proverbs	Jeremiah			Mark	1 Corinthians	
Leviticus	Ecclesiastes	Lamentations			Luke	2 Corinthians	
Numbers	Song of	Ezekiel			John	Galatians	
Deuteronomy	Solomon	Daniel				Ephesians	
						Philippians	
History and government		**Minor prophets**			**The early church**	Colossians	
						1 Thessalonians	
Joshua		Hosea			Acts	2 Thessalonians	
Judges		Joel				1 Timothy	
Ruth		Amos	The Old Testament looks forward to Christ's sacrifice on the cross.	The New Testament is based on the work Christ finished on the cross.		2 Timothy	
1 Samuel		Obadiah				Titus	
2 Samuel		Jonah				Philemon	
1 Kings		Micah					
2 Kings		Nahum				**General letters**	
1 Chronicles		Habakkuk				Hebrews	
2 Chronicles		Zephaniah				James	
Ezra		Haggai				1 Peter	
Nehemiah		Zechariah	About			2 Peter	
Esther		Malachi	400 years between testaments			1 John	
						2 John	
						3 John	
						Jude	
God used forty different men over a period of 1,500 years (about 1400 B.C. to A.D. 90) in writing the Bible.							

*From *Understanding the Bible* (London: Scripture Union, 1972), page 183.

3. How do the following verses describe God's word?

Matthew 24:35 _that God will not pass away_

John 17:17 _His word is truth_

Hebrews 4:12 _His word is sharper than a two edged sword_

4. Examine Psalm 19:7-11 carefully. Use the following chart to aid you in your investigation.

VERSE	WHAT THE BIBLE IS CALLED	ITS CHARACTERISTICS	WHAT IT WILL DO FOR ME
7	Law / Statutes	perfect / trustworthy	refreshes spiritually / gives wisdom
8	statutes	rejoicing	enlightens the eye
9		judgement	
10			
11			

In the chart above, place a check by the two or three thoughts which impressed you most about the Bible.

> *"It is the very nature and being of God to delight in communicating himself. God has no selfishness. God keeps nothing to himself. God's nature is to be always giving."*
> —ANDREW MURRAY*

HOW THE BIBLE HELPS YOU

5. Look up the following verses and summarize some of the ways the Bible is important to you as a Christian.

*From *Absolute Surrender* (Chicago: Moody Press, 1962), page 21.

16

875 Jeremiah 15:16 _____ day of SALVATION

1291 John 5:39 _____ that I will have eternal life

1544 2 Peter 1:4 _____ helps us to keep our focus on God and not the world

1352 1 John 2:1 _____ when we sin we can ask for forgiveness

6. Analogy is a form which explains something by comparing it point by point with something similar. In the following verses, what is God's word compared with? What is the function of these objects?

	OBJECT	FUNCTION
883 Jeremiah 23:29	Fire / Hammer	breaks it.
1150 Matthew 4:4	Bread/Word of God	feed us
1529 James 1:23-25	Law / mirror	to be a doer

✗ START   17 TH DARLTON + m ARTHUS

YOUR RESPONSIBILITY

7. "The Glories of God's Word" is a title given to Psalm 119. *1145* Nearly every verse of the psalm speaks of his word, and about applying it in daily living. Notice the psalmist's attitudes and actions concerning God's word. Beginning with verse 9, fill in the diagram below.

VERSE	ATTITUDE	ACTION
9	Want a Clean life	Keeping God's Word → pure life
10	Wholeheartedly sought God	Prayed – "Don't let me wander"
11	not to sin	Hid Word in his heart
12	praise	Asked God to teach him
13		With His lips he declared
14	Rejoice (Happy)	in His Testimonies
15	Self meditate	Contemplate
16	Delight	not going to forget

1296 8. According to John 8:31, what qualifies a man to be Christ's disciple?
1296 _____ To hold to His teachings

17

[handwritten at top:] If you know the truth the truth will set you free

How would you explain these words to another person?

[handwritten:] If you abide in the Lord you will be this disciple

9. From the following verses fill in the remaining blanks.

ACTION TO TAKE	WHY

650 Psalm 78:5-7 *[handwritten:]* To COMMAND Them TO TeLL THeIR ChiLDReN SO THey WOULDN'T Forget

1344 Acts 17:11 *[handwritten:]* RecIeve THe WORD, SeARch THe SCRIPTURes TO make SuRe IT WAS CORRect

1528 James 1:22 *[handwritten:]* Be DoeRS NOT HeARERS, SO you WONT Be DeCIeveD

1574 Revelation 1:3 *[handwritten:]* ReAD, HeAR, KeeP THe WORD, The TiMe IS NeAR

513 **10.** Ezra is a good example of a man who felt a responsibility toward God's word. What was his approach to Scripture?
Ezra 7:10 *[handwritten:]* Prepared his heart and to seek the law of the Lord and to teach the statutes and ordinances in Israel

Note the order of Ezra's actions. He applied the Scriptures to his own life before he taught them to others.

SCRIPTURE   EZRA   OTHERS

18

1462 **11.** Reflect carefully on Colossians 3:16. 2355

a. What practical steps can you take to allow Christ's word to dwell in you richly? (Examples: take notes during sermons; write out memory verses.)

(2) *Be in the word every day - Singing hymns - Praising the Lord - Praying and let our actions show our faith to others*

b. Number them in the order of effectiveness for yourself.
1. Prayer, being in the word, ...

c. During the next week, how can you put into practice the first two methods you numbered?

discipline ourself to do it

Romans 10:17 **Hear** 2234 2486
Revelation 1:3 **Read** 2180
Acts 17:11 **Study**
Psalm 119:9-11 **Memorize** 1195
Psalm 1:2-3 **Meditate** 1051

These five methods of Scripture intake help you get a firm grasp on God's word.

THE IMPORTANCE OF MEDITATION

Meditation on the Scriptures is prayerful reflection with a view to understanding and application. The goal is to conform your life to God's will by prayerfully thinking how to relate God's word to yourself.

19

12. From Joshua 1:8, answer the following questions.

a. What should be the source of your meditation?

The Bible

b. Briefly state the relationship between meditation
and application.

_Reading, understanding, memorizing
and living it._

c. What are the results of meditation? _Answer
to prayers - bring you closer to the
Lord_

13. Meditate on Psalm 1, and record your findings. Here are
some questions to help you get started:

How is the Christian like a tree?

What are the differences between the godly and the
ungodly man as to habits, stability, and future?

What new ideas from this psalm will help you in your relationship with God?

_By feeding (through the Word)
his is extended and bears
fruit by standing firm in your
belief._

_(the word - Seed to the Lord)
anyone in faith will prosper,
but those who don't will
perish._

_To bear the fruit of the
word to others._

20

In the space below, draw a simple picture that depicts the content of verses 2 and 3.

Remember These Points:

- God has communicated to man through his word— the Bible.
- Through the Scriptures you can get to know God better, understand his desires for your life, and discover new truths about living for him.
- God commands believers to let his word dwell richly in them. So it is important to give yourself wholeheartedly to allowing God's word to fill your life.
- God places emphasis on the act of meditating in his word, because effective meditation leads to personal application.

CHAPTER THREE

CONVERSING WITH GOD

Communication is essential for any growing relationship, including our relationship with God. Prayer is our means of communicating with him.

K 137

When you pray, the Holy Spirit helps you know what to say and how to say it (Romans 8:26-27).

> "*The Spirit links himself with us in our praying and pours his supplications into our own. We may master the technique of prayer and understand its philosophy; we may have unlimited confidence in the veracity and validity of the promises concerning prayer. We may plead them earnestly. But if we ignore the part played by the Holy Spirit, we have failed to use the master key.*"

> J. OSWALD SANDERS*

PRAYER—
YOUR COMMUNICATION
WITH GOD

K 151

1. As a believer in Christ you have been given a special opportunity, according to Hebrews 4:16. What is it and why was it given to you? *4:66*

THAT WE CAN COME BOLDY TU THE THRONE OF GR.

TU OBTAIN MERCY AND FIND GRACE IN THE TIM
OF NEED

*From *Spiritual Leadership* (Chicago: Moody Press, 1967), page 79.

K-637

2. Because God is the believer's refuge, what are you told to do? *Psalm 62:8* 898

TRUST HIM AT ALL TIMES AND POUR OUT YOUR HEARTS BEFORE HIM

K-1471 **How does 1 Thessalonians 5:17 relate to this verse?** 1841

WE ARE TO PRAY WITHOUT CEASING

3. Different types of prayer are necessary to communicate the variety of thoughts you want to express. Match each reference with the corresponding type of prayer.

K-619   K-1523   K-1528   K-1444
Psalm 38:18   *Hebrews 13:15*   *James 1:5*   *Ephesians 5:20*
877   879   *1 Samuel 12:23* 1880   1923
K-314
1315 Praise (for who God is) 1217 — EPHESIANS 5:20

Thanksgiving (for what he has done) — HEBREWS 13:15

Confession — PSALM 38:18

Prayer for others — 1 SAMUEL 12:23

Prayer for personal needs — JAMES 1:5

THE BENEFITS OF PRAYER

Not only do Christians have the privilege of talking with God about everything, they also experience great benefits from their communion with God.

4. What truth do you find both in Jeremiah 33:3 and Ephesians 3:20? 1820   K-894   1231   K-1444

HE WILL SHOW US GREAT AND MIGHTY THINGS THROUGH THE POWER THAT WORKS IN US

K-614 **5. What result did the psalmist experience when he prayed?** *Psalm 34:4* 871

HE WAS DELIVERED FROM ALL HIS FEARS

What are some fears you can discuss with God?

WITNESSING, WANTING All My FAMILY TO KNOW
JESUS, THE STATE OF our COUNTRY & WORLD
RETIRING

K1454 **6.** Paul wrote in Philippians 4:6-7 about a powerful key to
freedom from anxiety.   830

a. What are you to do? _Let your ReQuest Be MADE_

b. Why do you feel God is interested in every area of your life?

BeCAuse He IS ouR HeAVENly FATHER
AND He WATCHes OVeR His ChilVRen
He will NOT LeAve us OR FORSAke us

c. What is God's promise? _He will Give us PieCe AND_
UNDeR STANDING

d. In what area can you immediately begin to apply this truth?

HE HelPS me CONSTINTAlly Loith PRoBloMS AT WORK

CONDITIONS
OF PRAYER

7. What conditions of prayer do you find in the following
verses?   902
Psalm 66:18 _IF your HeART IS NOT RiGHT THe LorD will N_

K1176 Matthew 21:22 _HAve FAiTH + DO NOT DOuBT_
1532   You ASk WhAT you DeSiRe
K1305 John 15:7 _IF you ABiDe IN Him AND IT SHAll Be DONe FOR Y_
_1677_
K1310 John 16:24 _ASk AND Rfou will ReCieve THAT your Joy mAy Be_
_1679_
K1556 I John 5:14-15 _ASKING ACCORDiNG tO HiS will_
He will NeAR

Even when conditions are met, it sometimes appears as if God
is not answering prayer. But remember that "No" and
"Wait" are as much of an answer as "Yes."

1504

8. Consider Jesus' pattern for prayer in Matthew 6:9-13.

a. How does the prayer begin? Why is this important?

OUR FATHER   YOU ARE PRAYING TO GOD

b. Which requests are God-centered? YOUR KINGDOM COME,
THY WILL BE DONE, GIVE US THIS DAY

c. Which requests are man-centered? GIVE US THIS DAY
FORGIVE US OUR DEBTS, + DEBTORS

d. In what specific ways can this pattern for praying help you pray?

THAT WE DON'T ASK SELFISHLY FOR OUR
SELVES BUT THAT HIS WILL WILL BE DONE
IN ALL THINGS

JAN 5TH
2006

MARY
+
LARRY

**FOR WHOM
DO YOU PRAY?**

1378

9. What did Paul desire for those who didn't know Christ?
Romans 10:1 2233

THAT THEY WOULD BE SAVED

What did he do about it?

HE PRAYED FOR THEM

K1482

10. Read 1 Timothy 2:1-4. What groups of people should you pray for? Why? 2376

FOR THOSE IN AUTHORITY, THAT WE MAY
LEAD A QUIET + PEACEFUL LIFE IN ALL GODLINESS
AND REVERENCE. THIS IS ACCEPTABLE IN GODS
SIGHT WHO DESIRES ALL MEN TO BE SAVED AND
COME TO THE KNOWLEDGE OF THE TRUTH

11. What does the Lord desire you to pray for?
Matthew 9:37-38 /88 5

For THE LABORERS WhO TEACH &
PREACH HIS WORD

Why do you feel this is important?

Because THE WORLD IS full of
LOST PeoPle

12. How do you usually react when you have been intentionally mistreated by someone? Place an "X" by your first response.

X To become angry with him

___ To think of a way to get even

___ To make an excuse for him and try to forget it

(___ To pray for him)

___ To forgive but not forget

Other: _____

Examine Luke 6:28, then circle the correct response.
200 6   2328

13. Using Paul's prayer in Ephesians 3:14-21 as a guideline, list some requests you could pray for others and for yourself.

THAT HEARTS Be ReceptIve TO HIS Love
TO THE POINT OF ACCEPTING Jesus As SAVIOR

THAT I MAY Be STRENGTHENED IN HIS WORD
AND By HIS LUve TO Be A AMBASSITER
FOR Him WITHOUT FEAR

Have you been using a prayer list? A list can help you remember things you might otherwise forget to pray about. It can include:

- Your family
- Your non-Christian friends and acquaintances
- Your pastor and church
- Missionaries and Christian workers you know
- Those who oppose you
- Governmental authorities
- Your personal needs

DAILY CONVERSATION WITH GOD

14. What attitudes can you have in coming to God?

KG07 Psalm 27:8 *You SeeK THe LORD*

KG25 Psalm 46:10 *To EXALTe FHe LURD*

KG37 Psalm 63:1 *To AcKNowledge He IS GOD*

1097

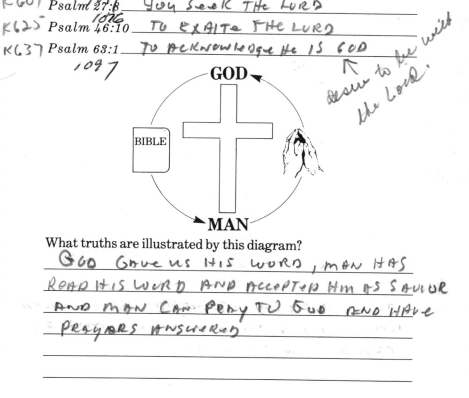

desire to be with the Lord.

What truths are illustrated by this diagram?

GOD GAVE US HIS WORD, MAN HAS READ HIS WORD AND ACCEPTED HIM AS SAVIOR AND MAN CAN PRAY TO GOD AND HAVE PRAYERS ANSWERED

2020

1253

15. Examine Luke 10:38-42. You can make several observations from this passage which relate to spending time with Jesus Christ.

a. Contrast the activities of Mary and Martha.

MARY	MARTHA
RESERVED	OUT GOING
PATIENT	IMPATIENT
EASY GOING	BUSY BODY

b. Which one did Jesus commend and why?

MARY, She chose THE GOOD PART
AND LISTENED TO JESUS

c. Like Martha, you may be easily distracted by many things. What activities might distract you from meeting with God?

SPORTS, WORK, family,
Being Tired

d. What can you do to overcome these distractions?

Need TO PUT Jesus AHead of
Pleasure

16. From what you have already learned in *Design for Discipleship*, record several reasons why you need to spend daily time with God—meditating on his word and conversing with him in prayer.

IT will Keep you Focused on Jesus
And By Being IN HIS WORD you will Learn
More each Time you Read. AND By
Praying you CAN See THE Results of
your PRAyers

28

Remember These Points:

- God has provided prayer as the means of communicating directly with him, through Jesus Christ.
- Prayer releases us from fear and worry.
- The Scriptures provide numerous patterns and examples for our prayer.
- God *desires* your fellowship, and you *need* to grow in your relationship with him. So regular times alone with God for the purpose of fellowship are vitally necessary.

CHAPTER FOUR

FELLOWSHIP WITH CHRISTIANS

"Accept life with humility and patience, generously making allowances for each other because you love each other. Make it your aim to be at one in the Spirit, and you will be bound together in peace. There is one Body and one Spirit, just as it was to one hope that you were called. There is one Lord, one faith, one baptism, one God and Father of us all, who is the one over all, the one working through all and the one living in all."

—EPHESIANS 4:2-6 (*PHILLIPS*)*

WHAT IS BIBLICAL FELLOWSHIP?

1. Read 1 John 3:1. If you are God's child and he is the Father of all, what does this tell you about your relationship to other believers?

they are your brothers and sisters in Christ

2. "Fellowship" is derived from the Greek word *koinonia*, which means "sharing in common." God has given you much to share. As you examine the verses on the next page, determine what you can share with others and one practical way to share it.

*From *The New Testament in Modern English, Revised Edition,* © 1958, 1960, 1972 by J. B. Phillips.

| WHAT TO SHARE | A WAY TO SHARE |

1 John 4:11, 21 _____ *Love* _____ *love one and*

Galatians 6:2 _____ *Burdens* _____ *Carrying each other*

Galatians 6:6 _____ *all good things* _____ *share with others*

James 5:16 _____ *Your Sins* _____ *Confess your*

3. Recall an incident when you were reluctant to allow someone to share something with you. Did your attitude hinder his
attempt at sharing? If so, how?

_____

_____

_____

_____

_____

Sharing involves giving and receiving, and both are integral
parts of meaningful fellowship.

4. Christians fellowship together on the basis of the fact that
they are forgiven sinners—forgiven, yes, but still sinners.
Knowing this fact, what is your responsibility toward your
brother when you have offended him? *Matthew 5:22-24*

to ask his forgiveness
Communion

_____

(*Raca* is a term expressing contempt for someone)

What is your responsibility when he has offended you?
Matthew 18:15,35

to show him his faults.
If he listens you have won
him over.

Christians can honestly share their lives. You don't have to
pretend to be something you are not.

31

5. Picture the following situation. Several Christians are in the same room drinking coffee and eating doughnuts as they discuss last week's championship game. The conversation moves to the subject of "which animal makes the best household pet." Then one of them tells a joke he recently heard. They enjoy a good laugh together, and begin to talk about the weather forecast for tomorrow. As one of them leaves, he says, "It sure is good to have Christian fellowship!"

a. Is this genuine Christian fellowship? _yes_

b. Why or why not? _they were fellowshipping together_

c. Could it be improved? How? _yes - things of the Lord could be there included_ _personal thing that the Lord has helped you or done for you -_

THE PURPOSE OF FELLOWSHIP

6. Why is fellowship important?

Proverbs 27:17 _keep every one strong_

Ecclesiastes 4:9-10 _one can strengthen the other (you can share your burden)_

7. What is the purpose of meeting together as believers?

Hebrews 10:24-25 _to encourage one another and build each other_

8. In studying a verse, it is often helpful to locate other verses elsewhere in the Bible which relate directly to the one being examined. The other verses are called *cross-references.* Hebrews 3:13 is a cross-reference to Hebrews 10:24-25. From this cross-reference, why is it necessary to encourage one another daily?

So that none of you will be hardened by sins deceitfulness

9. Explain why fellowship is important to you.

It keeps you in tune with other people

THE BODY OF CHRIST

10. God uses the analogy of a body to describe the relationship of believers with one another and with Christ. Who is the head of the body? Why? *Colossians 1:18*

Christ - He is the first born from the dead

11. Each believer is given different but important responsibilities in this spiritual body, the church. Read 1 Corinthians 12:14-27.

a. Who gave the members their various functions? *Verse 18*

God

b. What is his desire? *Verse 25* ___*that each part be created equally*___

c. What attitudes can lead to disharmony in the body?
Verses 15, 16, 21

you feel you are inferior

all parts fail

d. Are there any unnecessary functions (members) in the body? *Verses 20-22*

_no_

12. Think of what happens when you hit your finger with a hammer. How does this affect the entire body?

It brings pain

How can this illustration relate to the spiritual body?
1 Corinthians 12:26

they can suffer with it or rejoice with it

13. The body works together as one unit, yet it has many specialized organs which perform diverse functions. Summarize in a few sentences how both unity and diversity can exist together in the body.

14. According to Ephesians 4:2-3, what will preserve unity in the body? 2275

to be humble, gentleness, patience and loving one another in love

15. Examine your attitudes toward other Christians. Is there someone you find difficult to relate to in love as another member of Christ's body? Why?

Yes. They have a different attitude towards other Christians

What steps can you take to bring harmony to your relationship with this individual?

Go to the person and talk about it — or if you can't agree take two other people along with you

"How good and pleasant it is when brothers live together in unity!"

—PSALM 133:1

THE LOCAL CHURCH

16. What activities of the church in Jerusalem are mentioned in Acts 2:42? 2092

Teaching, breaking of Communion bread, and praying

Three distinguishing marks of the early church were:

(1) GENEROSITY   (2) PRAYER   (3) POWER

35

2276

17. Read Ephesians 4:11-13. Who is to equip (perfect) the saints so they can do the work of the ministry?

God

What is the ultimate goal of Christian ministry? *Verse 13*

To reach unity in faith, knowledge in the son of God and become mearture of the fullness of Christ

HE GAVE SOME TO BE...	APOSTLES PROPHETS EVANGELISTS PASTORS TEACHERS	TO PREPARE	GOD'S PEOPLE	FOR WORKS OF SERVICE, SO THAT	THE BODY OF CHRIST MAY BE BUILT UP

18. Examine 1 Peter 5:1-5. This passage gives direction to the leaders and members of a "flock." Using the following chart, contrast the right and wrong ways of demonstrating leadership. *Verses 2-3*

RIGHT WAY	WRONG WAY
Be Shepherds of God's Flock	
Not lording it over	
those entrusted to you	
Chief Shepherd	
Be Submissive	

What is your responsibility to your spiritual elders? *Verse 5*

To be submissive

36

19. In Colossians 4:3-4, Paul requested prayer for his ministry.

a. Paraphrase his request.

That he would proclaim the mystery of salvation clearly so everyone could understand it

b. Stop for a moment and use this request as a basis for praying for another Christian. Record the person's name here.

c. What is one thing you can do during this coming week to encourage those who are helping you walk with Christ?

Ask them to Pray for you.

20. What instructions are you given concerning the support of those who are appointed to preach and teach? 1 Corinthians 9:11,14   22:4

To help with their Physical needs.

Are you presently giving back to God part of what he is giving you? What does God want you to do with regard to prayer and financial support for your spiritual leaders?

Yes! To preach the gospel without charge

"Each Christian should select his church because he is convinced that within its particular structure he will find the greatest opportunities for spiritual growth, the greatest satisfactions for his human needs, and the greatest chance to be of helpful service to those around him."

—BILLY GRAHAM*

Remember These Points:

- Genuine fellowship is based on the concept of giving to and receiving from other Christians. You can share with others whatever God has given you—forgiveness, possessions, love, his word, and many other things.
- God gives fellowship for the purpose of mutual encouragement and growth.
- He wants Christians to live in unity and harmony with one another. To help us understand how believers are related, God uses the analogy of the body. Jesus Christ is the head of the body, which is comprised of all believers.
- All Christians throughout the world belong to Christ's body, but it is important for you to recognize how God wants you to be related to a smaller, specific group of believers. This smaller group is for the purpose of instruction, sharing, worship, and service. God has given spiritual leaders to help you mature in Christ and to become effective in the ministry.

*From *Peace with God* (New York: Doubleday, 1953), pages 177-178.

CHAPTER FIVE

WITNESSING FOR CHRIST

"It is the Holy Spirit, not we, who converts an individual. We, the privileged ambassadors of Jesus Christ, can communicate a verbal message; we can demonstrate through our personality and life what the grace of Jesus Christ can accomplish.... But let us never naively think that we have converted a soul and brought him to Jesus Christ.... No one calls Jesus Lord except by the Holy Spirit."

—PAUL LITTLE*

THE CHALLENGE

1. In Mark 5:18-19, notice Jesus' words to a man he had healed.

a. Where did he send him?

_____

b. What did he tell him to do?

_____

_____

c. Why do you suppose Jesus gave these particular instructions?

_____

*From *How to Give Away Your Faith* (Chicago: Inter-Varsity Press, 1966), page 53.

2. When you think about speaking of Christ, how do you react? (Either check a given sentence or write one of your own.)

___ I find it difficult to speak of such a personal matter.

___ I do not speak unless someone asks me.

___ I find it easy to talk to friends about Christ, but not people I don't know.

___ I find it easy to talk to strangers about Christ, but not close friends.

___ I often find myself talking to people about Christ, and I enjoy it very much.

_____

How do you think Peter would have answered this question? *Acts 4:20*

_____

_____

3. Sometimes you may feel as though you "need to know all the answers" before you can be an effective witness for Christ. What would you share with others? *1 John 1:3*

_____

_____

And for what purpose?

_____

_____

_____

How would you summarize the most important things you have seen and heard about Christ?

_____

_____

_____

_____

_____

4. Contrast the difference in the lives of the people in this chart:

	HOW DID THEY ACT?	WHY DID THEY ACT THIS WAY?
The Authorities (John 12:42-43)		
Paul (Romans 1:15-16)		

5. Carefully examine 2 Corinthians 5:9-14. In this section Paul lists several motivations and reasons for witnessing for Christ. List those you discover.

Verse 9 _____

Verse 10 _____

Verse 11 _____

Verse 14 _____

> *Witnessing is taking a good look at the Lord Jesus and then telling others what you've seen.*

HOW DO YOU BECOME AN EFFECTIVE WITNESS?

Witnessing is not merely an activity—it is a way of life. Christians don't *do* witnessing; they *are* witnesses—good or bad. Concentrate on improving your witness for Jesus Christ.

Witness by Love

6. Consider the qualities of love mentioned in 1 Corinthians 13:4-7. Which three do you feel would help you most to become a more effective witness for Christ?

_____

_____

_____

7. Read John 13:34-35. Imagine yourself as one of the apostles, and Jesus has just finished making this statement. What immediately comes to your mind?

_____

_____

Why do you think Jesus gave this command?

_____

_____

_____

Some people never read the Bible and seldom attend church. If you want them to know what Christ can do for them, let them see what Christ has done for you.

Witness by Life

8. What can be the results of your good works? *Matthew 5:16*

_____

9. Read 2 Corinthians 3:1-3. What did Paul say was true of the Corinthians?

_____

_____

Do you think people notice your life and consider it a witness for Jesus? Why or why not?

_____

_____

_____

_____

_____

"You are writing a gospel, a chapter each day,
by the deeds that you do and the words that you say.
Men read what you write—distorted or true;
What is the gospel according to you?"

—ANONYMOUS

Witness by Word

10. What challenge and instruction with regard to witnessing do you see in 1 Peter 3:15?

_____

_____

_____

_____

_____

_____

11. Paul gave some important facts about witnessing for Christ in 1 Corinthians 2:4-5. Paraphrase these verses.

_____

_____

_____

_____

_____

_____

_____

_____

12. The blind man whom Jesus healed had little or no theological training, but he was able to relate simply and effectively the facts of his experience. What did he say? *John 9:25*

_____

_____

_____

_____

Can you make a statement similar to that of the healed blind man? How would you say it in your own words?

_____

_____

_____

_____

> *"I cannot, by being good, tell men of Jesus' atoning death and resurrection, nor of my faith in his divinity. The emphasis is too much on me, and too little on him."*
>
> —SAMUEL SHOEMAKER*

PAUL'S STORY

Read the account of Paul's witness to King Agrippa and his royal party in Acts 26:1-29, then answer the following questions.

13. How did Paul begin his story? *Verses 2-3*

_____

14. What characterized his background? *Verses 4-5, 9-11*

_____

_____

(*Blaspheme* means to speak evil or contemptuously of God or sacred things)

15. What reversed the direction of Paul's life? *Verses 12-15*

_____

_____

16. How did Paul explain the gospel? *Verse 23*

_____

_____

*From *Extraordinary Living for Ordinary Men* (Grand Rapids, Michigan: Zondervan Books, 1965), page 117.

"Now, brothers, I want to remind you of the gospel I preached to you. . . . For what I received I passed on to you as of first importance: that Christ died for our sins according to the Scriptures, that he was buried, that he was raised on the third day according to the Scriptures."

—1 CORINTHIANS 15:1-4

17. What did Paul ask Agrippa? Why is this question important? *Verse 27*

_____

_____

_____

_____

_____

YOUR STORY

Now that you've seen how Paul gave his story, work on a way to tell yours. Sharing how you became a Christian can be one of the best ways of witnessing. It is particularly helpful in presenting Jesus Christ to relatives and close friends.

In sharing the story of your experience:

- Make it personal—don't preach. Tell what Christ has done for you. Use "I," "me," and "my"—not "you."
- Make it short. Three or four minutes should be enough time to cover the essential facts.
- Keep Christ central. Always highlight what he has done for you.
- Use the word of God. A verse or two of Scripture will add power to your story. Remember that the word of God has a keen cutting edge.

How to Prepare Your Story

Try writing your story down on the next page just the way you would tell it to an unbeliever. Make the story clear enough that the person hearing it would know how to receive Christ.

Tell a little about your life before you trusted Jesus Christ; then about your conversion, how you came to trust him; and finally something of what it has meant to know him—the bless-

45

ing of sins forgiven, assurance of eternal life, and other ways your life or outlook has changed

If you have been a Christian for a number of years, be sure that your story includes some current information about the continuing effect of Christ in your life.

As you prepare your story, ask the Lord to give you opportunities to share it. Pray for two or three whom you would particularly like to tell about Jesus Christ in your neighborhood, at work, or at school, and take the first opportunity to share your story with them.

MY
STORY

Before I trusted Christ:

How I trusted Christ:

Since I've trusted Christ:

In conclusion, remember that you do not have the power in yourself to convince anyone of spiritual truth. The Holy Spirit convicts non-Christians of their need to know Christ (John 16:8). As you pray for those with whom you desire to share your story, be sure to ask God to honor the proclamation of his word, to convince people of their need, and to strengthen you as you share the gospel.

Remember These Points:

- According to the principles of Scripture, we are to be witnesses of what we see and hear of Christ.
- We are witnesses by actions of love, by our lifestyle, and by our speech.
- Paul's spoken testimony provides a pattern for verbal witness: telling what our life was like before we met Christ, telling how we met Christ, and telling what our life is like since meeting him.

WE HAVE A STUDY THAT'S RIGHT FOR YOU.

Whether you're a new believer wanting to know the basics of Christianity, a small-group leader building new groups, or someone digging deeper into God's Word, we have something for you!

From topical to inductive, NavPress studies emphasize in-depth spiritual change for believers at all levels. Each contains a combination of questions, tools, Scripture, leader's guides, and other materials for groups or individuals. If you want to study a book of the Bible, learn to handle stress, be a good parent, or communicate effectively with God, we have the resources for your Bible study needs.

Why go anywhere else?

To get your copies, visit your local bookstore, call 1-800-366-7788, or log on to www.navpress.com. Ask for a FREE catalog of NavPress products. Offer BPA.

NAVPRESS
BRINGING TRUTH TO LIFE
www.navpress.com